THE SEVEN HABITS OF HIGHLY INEFFECTIVE PEOPLE

The
Seven Habits
of
Highly Ineffective People

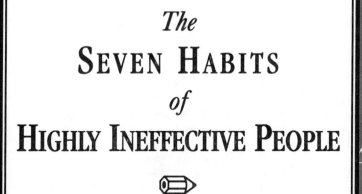

Low Effort Lessons in
Mismanaging for Success

Herman Minor IV

A Citadel Press Book
Published by Carol Publishing Group

A Citadel Press Book
Published by Carol Publishing Group
Citadel Press is a registered trademark of Carol Communications, Inc.
Editorial Offices: 600 Madison Avenue, New York, N.Y. 10022
Sales and Distribution Offices: 120 Enterprise Avenue, Secaucus, N.J.
07094
In Canada: Canadian Manda Group, P.O. 920, Station U, Toronto,
Ontario M8Z 5P9
Queries regarding rights and permissions should be addressed to
Carol Publishing Group, 600 Madison Avenue, New York, N.Y. 10022

Carol Publishing Group books are available at special discounts for
bulk purchases, for sales promotions, fund-raising, or educational
purposes. Special editions can be created to specifications. For
details, contact Special Sales Department, Carol Publishing Group,
120 Enterprise Avenue, Secaucus, N.J. 07094

Designed by Jessica Shatan

Manufactured in the United States of America
10   9   8   7   6   5   4   3   2   1

Library of Congress Cataloging-in-Publication Data
Mount, Franklin M.
       The seven habits of highly ineffective people: low effort
lessons in mismanaging for success / by Herman Minor, IV.
          p. cm.
       "A Citadel Press book."
       ISBN 0-8065-1582-1
       1. Management. 2. Success in business. 3. Management–Humor.
I. Title.
HD38.M523 1994   94-20355
658.4--dc20   CIP

After finding no qualified candidates for the position of principal, the school department is extremely pleased to announce the appointment of David Steele to the post.
—PHILIP STREIFER,
  Superintendent of Schools,
  Barrington, Rhode Island

CONTENTS

The Seven Habits—A Study in Contrast

You may be aware of the mega-bestseller, *The Seven Habits of Highly Effective People*, by Stephen R. Covey. However, if you're reading this book, which you must be if you're reading this, then you probably haven't read—and, more important, have no intention whatsoever of reading—Stephen Covey's book.

Don't get me wrong. I don't dislike Covey's book. I suppose it has its uses—it certainly makes sense on its own terms.

My goal with *The Seven Habits of Highly Ineffective People* is not to poke fun at or demean Covey, his book, or his message.

My intention is much more basic than that. I intend to construct a framework of ineffectiveness. In this way, those of us who will never be effective can go on pretending to work in the face of increasing demands for responsibility, performance, and, yes, effectiveness.

Think of my book as the book for those of us who should read Stephen Covey's masterpiece—*but will not!*

The diagram below illustrates how three fundamental needs—security, laziness, and income—intersect to form ineffectiveness.

Throughout this book, I will use simplistic, ordinary, and seemingly worthless diagrams, charts, and tables—constructed from simple, interchangeable symbols—as visual aids for my ineffective principles. These both help you to get through the book without having to read too many words

Laziness
(You)

Ineffective
Habits

Security
(No Worry)

Income
(Survival)

Ineffectiveness
(Acquired Tactics and Ruses)

and help you *understand* the book without having to think too much.

Each of the parts and each of the chapters also begins with a quote, which my underpaid and overworked research staff has culled from various unremarkable sources.

A Contrast

COVEY	MINOR
PART ONE Paradigms and Principles	PART ONE Surviving the Performance- Driven Culture *Why I Wrote This Book*
PART TWO Private Victory	PART TWO The Self
HABIT 1 Be Proactive *Principles of Personal Vision*	HABIT 1 Be Reactive *Avoid Both Commitment and* *Responsibility*
HABIT 2 Begin With the End in Mind *Principles of Personal Leadership*	HABIT 2 Procrastinate *Protect Leisure Time on and Off* *the Job*
HABIT 3 Put First Things First *Principles of Personal* *Management*	HABIT 3 Don't Waste Time Setting Priorities *Avoid the Trap of Effective Time* *Management*
PART THREE Public Victory: Paradigms of Interdependence	PART THREE Helping the Self

Part One

WHY I WROTE THIS BOOK

SURVIVING THE PERFORMANCE-DRIVEN CULTURE

If they're so great, how come they're running this company?
—OVERHEARD IN AN OFFICE

It's no secret that in America today we face problems of great magnitude. These include uncompetitive industries, declining educational standards, rising deficits, urban decay, skyrocketing teenage pregnancies and drug use, spiraling crime rates, and war. (Actually, there is no war at the moment, but it is always a possibility.)

In addition, there is a movement on for "effectiveness." People are supposed to *justify* their salaries, perks, and business practices *on the basis of how well they work!* This is shocking, dismaying, and frightening for anyone who has built an ineffective career.

That's where I come in. I am an ineffective consultant. Once, I was an ineffective management trainee, following my ineffective (and largely forgotten) college career. I moved up the ladder, by changing companies frequently and moving around the country to stay ahead of my reputation, and became an ineffective but very well paid executive. Now I provide advice that either is useless or tells companies and their people how to be useless—and *ineffective*.

But first, let's look at some basic issues.

The first question is, how does an ineffective individual function in this threatening environment?

Let's look at some incorrect ways. There are a lot of people who focus on improving themselves: developing new skills, increasing self-esteem, and paying serious attention to their work and lives. *This book is not for them.* This book is for those of us—*and we know who we are*—who have neither the time nor the inclination for such activities.

Before we may proceed and look at the correct ways of functioning in today's threatening business world, we must ask ourselves a fundamental question: *Why do we work?*

To make money.

Of course, there are many different ways to make money, but work—of some sort—is the only option open to most of us. Criminality can produce income, but the downside is truly nasty. Prison sucks, in a nutshell. There are, it is true, ineffective criminals who only get probation or who go to "white-collar" prisons. Generally, however, these white-collar criminals *already had a job.* Why jeopardize a perfectly good ineffective niche just to steal a few more dollars?

Entrepreneurship is another way to pull in an income. The virtues of entrepreneurship are highly touted, but do you have any idea *how difficult it is to run a business?* Do you know how long the hours are?

Clearly, for the ineffective millions, entrepreneurship is out of the question. In fact, entrepreneurs are themselves usually driven, discontented, and even *demanding* people. These traits make them difficult to work for—and are certainly not ineffective traits at all.

For these reasons, I recommend avoiding entrepreneurship as well as entrepreneurs, even socially. (One minor exception: Daydreaming about ideas for businesses can be a pleasant diversion as well as a good way to occupy time at work.)

Another avenue to an income is through what some call "creativity." Write a book, a screenplay, or a television script (also known as a "teleplay," which is not the same as staying at home and playing Wheel of Fortune along with Pat and Vanna). While this is not an easy path to ineffectiveness, it holds some promise.

Any publisher or producer can regale you with stories of woefully ineffective writers, some of whom are world-class passive-aggressives. These careers can also be quite lucrative, although they usually are not. Less than five percent of "writers" make a living from their writing. *The rest have real jobs!* Not only that, many of those jobs are truly thankless ones, like waiter or legal proofreader, which, even worse, allow little room for ineffectiveness.

In general, I recommend staying away from the so-called "creative" fields. (One exception: If you develop great ineffectiveness in a particular specialty, you may be able to hire someone to write your book for you, paying them only a small fraction of the advance and any additional royalties that may accrue. For many ineffectives—from businesspeople to psychologists to presidential-offspring mystery writers—this practice has proved lucrative. And, in truly ineffective fashion, you have to just fall into it.)

By far the best way to make an income is simply to collect an income. The problem with this method is that it is basically open only to those who have inherited wealth—that is, this method depends on an accident of birth. As Malcolm Forbes once sagely remarked, "The secret of getting rich is choosing the right parents."

There is, however, one way to get around this basic fact of life: *Marry the rich*. If you are very attractive, perhaps servile, and certainly socially sophisticated (by this I do *not* mean socially conscious), marrying the rich is a real alternative. There are even classes and books on the subject. This method is especially suited to people who *seem* to have a personality, but don't. Marrying the rich generally involves a bit of bending, bowing, and scraping, which is not the end of the world. Some people even get off on it.

As noted previously, however, the sad fact is that most of us cannot pursue these paths, however much we fantasize about them. Most of us must work, and work is a bitch. "Work Sucks," reads a noted T-shirt.

Let's face the facts. Not everyone can be head of a major corporation, a doctor, a lawyer (although many lawyers need not read this book and are in fact superb practitioners of ineffectiveness), or even a veterinarian.

Most of us ineffectives now work in unnecessary middle management jobs of the sort which are under fire today. Most of us worry about our jobs, and with good reason: In an era of rising performance standards, we may well *deserve* to be fired.

Downsizing, right-sizing, "reengineering," and other trends in corporate America threaten the security of millions of Americans. Why? Because the rocket scientists who run these companies have botched their jobs. Now they're trying to protect their paychecks by taking ours away.

I see this book as a call to arms for those scared people who constitute the ineffective millions. Why should we lose our jobs and livelihoods just because our overpaid bosses want to keep theirs?

America is a democracy, and in a democracy, everyone has rights and everyone has a place. If current trends continue, democracy itself will be endangered. After all, democracy is an ineffective form of government, which is what makes it great.

The KGB was a very *effective* organization that stopped at nothing to achieve its goals. The many spy scandals of the last few years—most recently the Aldrich Ames case, which also exposed the ineffectiveness of the extremely well funded CIA (a former consulting client of Minor Associates) prove this.

Now more and more corporations are practicing KGB-like tactics such as monitoring job performance and maintaining detailed records. But, after you have read this book and absorbed its lessons, you will turn these weapons back on your corporation—and your colleagues—and *increase your income* while *decreasing your workload*.

You'll love yourself for it—in more ways than one!

I'm not saying that this book can solve your problems. In fact, *by definition*, it cannot. It can, however, help guide you through the minefields of corporate America and provide you with the tools necessary to *seemingly accidentally* carve out a well-paying niche as a highly ineffective person.

Read this book and you will be on your way to *the invaluable career track of failing upward*.

Each of the parts and chapters that follow starts out with what I call the "Pyramid of Ineffectiveness." At the bottom

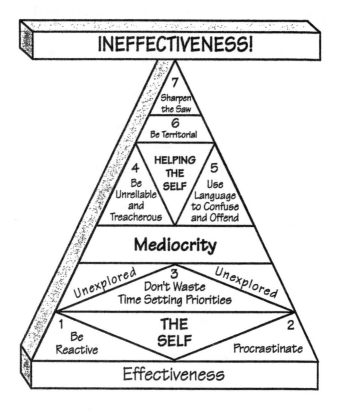

The Pyramid of Ineffectiveness

is "Effectiveness," which is where many of us, brainwashed by society, begin. All of the habits fit together, and as you progress through the book, you will move through the habits to "Mediocrity" and, eventually, top out in "INEFFECTIVENESS!"

One final point: As you will note, this is a short book. To write a long one would be against my principles.

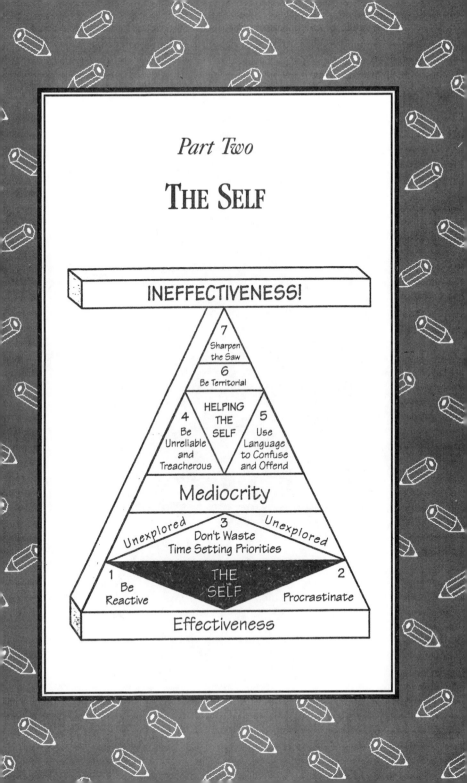

Part Two

THE SELF

INEFFECTIVENESS!

7
Sharpen
the Saw

6
Be Territorial

HELPING
THE
SELF

4
Be
Unreliable
and
Treacherous

5
Use
Language
to Confuse
and Offend

Mediocrity

Unexplored

3
Don't Waste
Time Setting Priorities

Unexplored

1
Be
Reactive

THE
SELF

2
Procrastinate

Effectiveness

Nice guys finish seventh.
—LEO DUROCHER

This part, encompassing Habits 1, 2, and 3, is entitled "The Self"—with good reason. Its subject is *the self*. Quite simply, you must concentrate on yourself to even begin to have a chance at true ineffectiveness. Ineffectiveness begins at home.

The basis of these first three habits is passing the buck. The buck *must not* stop at your desk. When you have read and put into practice these habits and their underlying tactics and strategies, you will have increased—massively—your ineffectiveness and your happiness.

You will be working less and living more—and perhaps even climbing the corporate ladder. You certainly won't be falling. Others may fall because of you, but that's not your problem. In fact, it's to your benefit, as long as those displaced are not your comrades in ineffectiveness.

The twin pillars of passing the buck are *reacting appropriately to threats* and *setting traps for others*. See the illustration below.

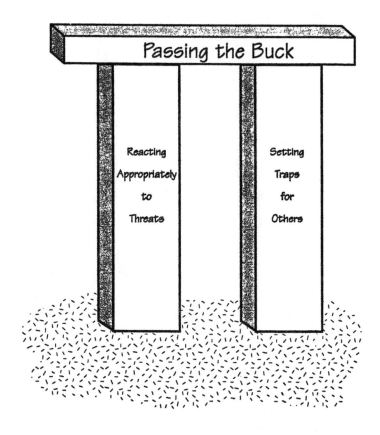

You must be ready and willing to shamelessly cover up any and all screwups on your part—both of omission and commission. I will outline both active and passive ways of doing this.

At times, you will have to take action to save your paycheck, or at least your facade of pride. At other times—and this is beautiful—you will be able to force others to save you. Sometimes these people will hurt themselves in the process. This is even better than backstabbing. I call it "induced career suicide."

The three habits in this part are:

1. Be reactive
2. Procrastinate.
3. Don't waste time setting priorities.

These habits overlap and mutually reinforce one another, as do all truly ineffective habits, techniques, tactics, and strategies. Together, they form a Wall of Confusion that you can employ in your drive to become ever more ineffective.

| 1 | 2 | 3 |
| Be Reactive | Procrastinate | Don't Waste Time Setting Priorities |

Wall of Confusion

1. *Be reactive*. This habit requires some explanation. It involves more than simple involuntary reflexes. There is nothing worse than a knee-jerk ineffective. While ineffectiveness requires a profound aversion to real work, it also requires guile and, once in a while, effort.

In short, you have to do more than merely deal with problems when they arise. You must assiduously deflect responsibility, not merely cover up problems. I outline several basic methods for doing exactly this.

2. *Procrastinate*. You may wonder why this habit is so close to the front of the book. Shouldn't it be put off to later? No! Procrastination itself is *not* something you put off. Procrastination is the act of putting *other* things off. Under this habit, I note how I have put off developing a complete, unified theory of procrastination. *That* is procrastination.

The crux of my case is that procrastination can reduce actual work and responsibility without hindering your career.

Procrastinate your way to success—the ineffective way!

3. *Don't waste time setting priorities*. This is the final habit of this first part. It is, of course, a cousin to Habit 2. Its heart and soul is understanding the illusory nature of time.

All of our lives, we are bombarded with the notion that time is of great value. "Time is of the essence." (What in the hell does that mean?) "There's no time to lose." We've heard them all, but the fact is, time is time. *The way to make time go by is by not working.* ("My, how times flies!")

Of course, it is impossible to totally avoid work. One can, however, minimize work time and thus maximize leisure time—on and off the job. I will outline some tried-and-true basic points to mismanaging time—the bricks that make up the path to true ineffectiveness.

If you use time effectively, you will increase your utility to your colleagues and, even worse, to your employer. Your purpose is to help yourself. To know life, you must focus on yourself—not on others.

In the workplace, as in all parts of life, you have to focus on your own wants and needs first. Other people matter only to the extent that you can use them to get your way. There is a lot of denial about this fact in our society (in fact, throughout human history), but it is the unvarnished existential truth.

For example, I am writing this book for money. I don't care if you're able to use it or not—*or even if you can read it or not*—as long as you *pay* for it. Of course, I hope to both protect and spread ineffectiveness, but that is mainly to make my own ineffectiveness less apparent. It is a less important selfish reason than money.

The imperative to be an ineffective selfish bastard carries several distinct meanings. First of all, you must visualize yourself at the center of the world. Second, you must value your lack of responsibility and commitment to others. Third, you must learn the invaluable skills of covering your ass and laying blame on others. Finally, you must learn to drift from problem to problem without either seeming lazy or, even worse, solving these problems. *People who consistently solve problems often solve their way into unemployment.*

Habit 1: Be Reactive

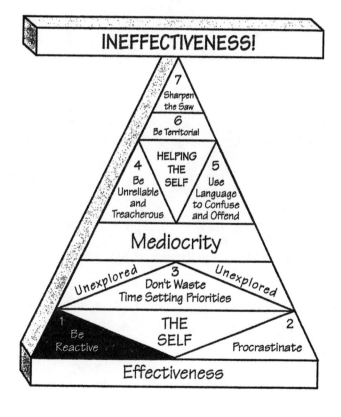

AVOID BOTH COMMITMENT
AND RESPONSIBILITY

*The President is aware of what is going on. That's not to
say there is something going on.*
—RON ZIEGLER,
  Press Secretary to President Richard Nixon

"Commitment." "Responsibility." These are highly
esteemed words in our society. Truthfully, though,
how often do we see them put into practice?

The answer is seldom. Commitment and responsibility may
be vital to the smooth and effective functioning of society,
but we're not talking about that here. We're talking about
ineffectiveness, and for the ineffective, it is necessary to
avoid both commitment and responsibility—while seeming
to uphold both!

If you look at the highest levels of society, you will see that
artifice rules the day. In Congress, in the executive branch,
in the judiciary (how I envy the leisure-filled day of a judge!)
and in state and local government, *avoidance is the norm.*

I don't even need to go into the hundreds of billions of dollars our greatest corporations spend to cover up their ineffectiveness. There are *fabulous* opportunities for ineffectiveness in public relations. Of course, the ineffectiveness found at the highest levels of business and government is beyond the scope of this book—but it is *inspirational*.

Without a doubt, much of government bureaucracy offers excellent opportunities for ineffectiveness. Even better are state and local governments, most of which are wonderfully ineffective—and filled with ineffective people who revel in ineffectiveness.

Unfortunately, the vast majority of jobs are in the private sector, and, *sadly*, most ineffective people will have to find their way working outside of government. For the fortunate few who can achieve civil service status, the wisdom of this book will become second nature.

For most of the ineffective population, however, a continuous reexamination of the Seven Habits will be necessary.

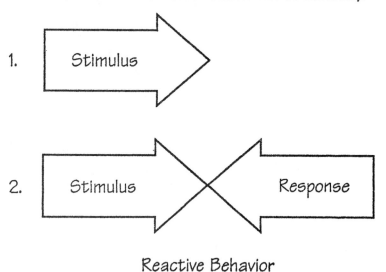

Reactive Behavior

This is okay. As long as you follow the spirit of ineffective-ness, you will prosper to a surprising, indeed *amazing*, extent.

The basic idea of reactive behavior is shown by the diagram on the previous page.

As you can see, you simply wait until a problem arises. Then you react against it. *Anybody can do that.*

In my career as an ineffective mismanagement consultant, I have found four basic principles to avoiding commitment and responsibility:

> • Be vague, but demand precision.
> • Document everything, or fake it later.
> • When you screw up, require your subordinates to fix the problem. (Don't fix it yourself under any cir-cumstances.)
> • Hoard important information.

Let's examine these principles of paradox—counterintuitive ineffective wisdom, if you will—in some detail:

Be vague, but demand precision. This approach is vitally important for those who wish to maximize the utility of their subordinates to reduce their own workload. When giving assignments, provide only the most basic data. *Consciously withhold important but not absolutely essential information*. This can range from telephone numbers to basic procedures. *Don't make things unnecessarily straightforward.*

Finding out basic procedures and information will not only occupy your subordinates' time, hindering their performance and thereby protecting your own ineffectiveness, it will also annoy them. Annoyed people are annoying to others, and this will make them less popular in the organization.

Because their tasks will be more difficult—and because of the lack of respect you are showing—your subordinates will produce lower-quality work. Now you can zapp them by pointing out the imprecision and simple errors in their product. This will give you someone to blame as well as keep them down. In other words, you will have created a *designated scapegoat*.

An added benefit is the increased turnover that results. This reduces the likelihood of your developing dangerously effective underlings.

Document everything, or fake it later. This is a corollary to the famous C.Y.A. ("cover your ass") dictum. This habit is unquestionably one of the most ineffective practices in corporate America. Untold *millions* of working hours are wasted by "carboning" people (in itself a delightfully anti-quated term) and documenting activity—*or inactivity* (which I prefer).

All this happens because recordkeeping allegedly increases accountability. In reality, nothing could be further from the truth. One must keep records, of course, but recordkeeping is easily manufactured or manipulated.

Simply create new documents and backdate them. It takes the equivalent of a criminal investigation to uncover backdating, and that's not going to happen unless criminality is involved. And, as I demonstrated earlier, criminality is a poor path to ineffectiveness.

When you screw up, require your subordinates to fix the problem. (Don't fix it yourself under any circumstances.) This is a basic tactic of ineffectiveness which ineffective people often miss. Trying to prevent scrutiny of a mistake, which is usually of the most obvious and egregious nature, we often try to fix the mistake without anybody knowing.

While this is a laudable instinct, it is almost always doomed to failure and is ultimately self-defeating. Have your subordinates fix the problem—but don't explain the cause. In fact, it is best to "cleanse" the relevant files, leaving a big puzzle. This will occupy their time and drive them crazy. *The really beautiful part of this stratagem is that they will take the blame, should the screwup come to the attention of higher-ups.* Again, *you have created a designated scapegoat.* Now be sure to create a new paper trail. This will permanently obscure the truth and deflect responsibility.

Hoard important information. Of all the principles of avoiding commitment and responsibility, this one is perhaps the most important. There is much in the media about how we now live in an "information age" and that America's economy is becoming "information-based."

If you are ineffective, you probably have not read anything about this, but you most likely have heard about it while flipping from station to station while looking for some narcotic television viewing.

Most of us don't know what these pronouncements mean. And with good reason—every age has been "information-based." What is the purpose of language but to communicate information (or mis- and disinformation)? Ever since there have been people, we have been living in an "information-based" society. When a cave-man father taught his caveboy son to carve arrowheads and build fires, he was imparting information.

It becomes clear, then, that *if you hold information that others need, you have an advantage.* All societies have been based on certain classes' restricting others' access to information. For example, under European feudalism, the knights kept the peasants from knowing how to use swords and ride horses. In Japan, the samurai did the same thing, and they didn't even allow peasants to learn how to read. In order to preserve their status, they outlawed guns. Talk about ineffective! *The peasants did the work!* Without these examples, we would not have George Will!

Today, managers at each level withhold information from those below them. If they didn't, there would be no rationale for their holding their positions. It's as simple as that.

Recently, management theories attacking uncommunicativeness and control freaks in general have been gaining popularity. This trend must be covertly and deviously resisted. When you hear such words as "boundarylessness," "empowerment," or, even worse, "team performance," you know something is going very wrong. This is when you must dig in your heels and fight back through sabotage, backstabbing, and the like. More on this later.

CASE STUDY

A *"Damage Control" Executive for an Oil Company*

A good friend and "behind-the-scenes personal consulting client" is named Richard, but I'll call him Billy here. He is very well paid and gets to travel all over the world for his work—because his company *is* all over the world—in more ways than one.

Thor Heyerdahl remarked, after his voyage across the Atlantic Ocean in a reed boat (twenty-three years after the voyage of the *Kon Tiki*, which took place in some other ocean), that even weeks away from land, in water two or three *miles* deep, that tarry blobs of oil were ubiquitous— that is, all over the place.

Billy and his colleagues secretly take this as a compliment. Oil is big. (And why was Heyerdahl traveling in a reed boat, anyway, when oil-powered ships are available? Ostensibly, to show that Africans could have crossed the Atlantic and influenced the Mayan civilization. That's nice. Really, he is an antiprogress fanatic.)

Well, as you can imagine, the *biggest, dirtiest, and most important business in the world* offers plenty of opportunities for damage control experts. And with this kind of money at stake, you better believe that Billy is well compensated.

The beautiful thing about Billy's job is that it requires no planning. *You can't plan*—disasters happen when they feel like it.

You can react, however. You fly in, survey the damage, and look for bright spots.

"It's not as bad as it looks."

"We're learning how better to deal with spills."

"The captain was drunk."

Billy dreams up steps that his company has allegedly already taken and distributes them to the media. He puts out figures on how much money the company is spending on the cleanup. He praises volunteer efforts, but calls for more cooperation from the environmentalists. Above all else, he protects his bosses from scrutiny.

Meanwhile, Billy's superiors, who do plan ahead from time to time (in a slap dash way), are calling in political favors from ineffective politicians whom they finance—in whatever country you're talking about. I don't have to tell you how helpful this is down the line.

You're going to take a beating in the media. *Billy doesn't take it personally—it's their job.* Many in the media are also ineffective. Billy's job is to react to these beatings and put out the company's line, which is a bit like the Wall of Confusion I mention and illustrate at the beginning of this part.

What you *don't want* is *more regulation* and the governmental *expectation of responsibility.*

Billy is living quite well, thank you, and his employer's stock is higher than ever. What more could you ask?

Ineffectiveness may be easy, but it's not simple. It does require effort, just a lot less effort than effectiveness. But you are already on the way to a conscious understanding of what were previously subconscious bad work habits. If you keep on, you will learn more of the invaluable secrets of failing upward.

HABIT 2: PROCRASTINATE

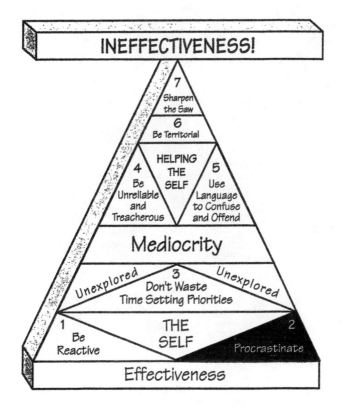

INEFFECTIVENESS!

7
Sharpen
the Saw

6
Be Territorial

4
Be
Unreliable
and
Treacherous

HELPING
THE
SELF

5
Use
Language
to Confuse
and Offend

Mediocrity

Unexplored

3
Don't Waste
Time Setting Priorities

Unexplored

1
Be
Reactive

THE
SELF

2
Procrastinate

Effectiveness

PROTECT LEISURE TIME
ON AND OFF THE JOB

In the last twenty years, the amount of time Americans have spent at their jobs has risen steadily. Each year the change is small...but the accumulated increase over two decades is substantial. The shrinkage of leisure has created a profound crisis....Despite these obstacles, I am hopeful.
—JULIET B. SCHOR, *The Overworked American*

One of the great problems facing America and Americans today is the erosion of leisure time. What is life for? Work? Achievement? Don't make me laugh. (Actually, *do* make me laugh, but not with that joke.)

Life is to be enjoyed. Why did nature give us the capacity to revel in pleasure? And what is the most dependable source of pleasure after sleep? (Sex, while usually better than sleep, is seldom dependable.) *Loafing,* of course.

There is a dangerous idea which is spreading in America today: Employment should require work. While this may be true in a few professions (which escape me at the moment), it is in general untrue. The evidence is all around, but I have neither the time nor, more important, the inclination to go into it here.

If you're reading this book, I'm sure you don't need tips on leisure time during your actual time at home. I'm sure your living space is a mess, with the possible exception of somewhat clear paths connecting the sofa, bed, refrigerator, bathroom, and television. (Or maybe you have an overworked and underpaid housekeeper.)

What is increasingly a challenge today is *minimizing time at work* and, on top of that, *minimizing work time at work.* Helping you realize those two ambitions is the thrust of this chapter.

I cannot offer a complete, unified framework of procrastination. That's a major task which I've been planning. However, I still haven't gotten around to it. There's a lesson in that fact.

The diagram on the next page shows the *process* of procrastination. Stimulus leads to confusion, which leads to the death of the stimulus.

Let me offer some concrete, or at least muddy, strategies of work avoidance:

- Arrive late and make it look like you're on time.
- Use your computer to pretend to work.
- Make personal phone calls look like business calls.
- Leave work early consistently and cover it up.

These are stunning methods of artful laziness. Pay attention, if only for a few minutes.

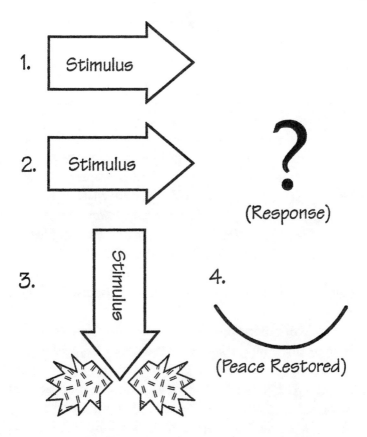

1. Stimulus

2. Stimulus

?

(Response)

3. Stimulus

4.

(Peace Restored)

The Process of Procrastination

Arrive late and make it look like you're on time. This is the cornerstone of minimizing time at work, since it reduces the total time spent at work without cutting into official, *paid*, time at work. Do this right, and you'll be well on your way to creative loafing.

There are several basic rules to follow. First of all, arrive on time at least once or twice a week. (I'm so sorry to have to include this unfortunate piece of advice.) The best days to do this are Tuesdays or Wednesdays. Mondays everyone is too depressed to notice—even if they're on time, they're not yet mentally at work.

Thursdays and Fridays, however, are permissible late days, especially Fridays. If you work at a company with real party animals, everyone will have a hangover on Friday, since Thursdays really start the weekend. And, since the habit of leaving early on Friday for the weekend escape has caught on, Fridays have become especially good for late arrivals.

A late arrival combined with an early departure, a long "wet" lunch, and dilatory work while you are actually at work, produces a day of minimal strain—and maybe even substantial pleasure.

It's almost as good as the weekend. Fridays, properly utilized, can make for fine leisure days disguised as work days.

A couple of other tips:

If you come in especially late, hide your bag and/or coat before walking to your office. Usually there is a supply closet or empty office which will serve well for this purpose. You will appear to have already been hard at work and simply returning from the bathroom or a quick errand to a vending machine or newsstand.

Another possibility is to impose on the receptionist—but ingratiate yourself first. An angry receptionist can be a powerful source of gossip. You want to gossip about others, not be a source of gossip.

Also, require your assistant to turn on your office light— when he or she arrives *on time.*

Use your computer to pretend to work. This is an invaluable skill. If you are typing away, eyes intently focused on your monitor, and all you're doing is pretending to work, you'll be very ineffective. You can embellish or edit and reedit memos and reports in spurious backup files. When you're done, destroy the backup file and turn in the original, simple, and perhaps even to-the-point version. (I realize that this is dangerously close to effectiveness, but at least you *wasted time* doing it.)

There are also computer games that you can load into your computer for office use. Two of my favorites are "Solitaire" and "Sim-City." Sim-City is particularly time-consuming, although it is rather difficult. WARNING: Don't allow your monitor to face your office door if you employ this technique.

Make personal phone calls look like business calls.
This requires some diligence and attention, since personal phone calls are to be enjoyed and business calls are to be avoided.

You will, in time, develop your own style at this, so I'll just give you a few recommendations. First of all, *lean forward* while on the phone. During personal phone calls, the tendency is to lean back—that is, to kickback and enjoy yourself. Don't. Lean forward.

Secondly, have work papers or note pads in front of you on your desk. *Pretend to look at these.* Occasionally move your eyes and shift the papers, perhaps even scribble something down.

Next, *throw in a few work-related sentences* from time to time. These will shield you against eavesdroppers *and* provide humor for the conversation, since the other person will pick up on what you're doing.

Another possibility is to actually *schedule personal phone calls.* This is fantastic fun, and not as difficult as you might think. You can interrupt meetings and other dreary work-related activities by taking a significant look at your watch and saying, "I've got an important phone call now." It *is* important, but not to work!

Leave work early consistently and cover it up. This skill is literally the capstone of an ineffective day at work. There are innumerable excuses for leaving early, ranging from concocted doctor's appointments to work-related errands out of the office. These are all good in their own way, but a detailed and lengthy exposition of them and their relative merits and drawbacks is totally beyond the scope of this slim volume.

One particularly useful technique is to leave your desk casually cluttered and to stash your coat and/or bag in the lobby or another location. This way, you can casually walk out as if you're going to get a cup of coffee or take a well-deserved cigarette break.

Later, when you're at home (or at a bar or restaurant with a few quiet phone booths), call in to your voice mail and retrieve your messages. Answer any that you can, or at least return the phone calls to the other person's voice mail. Most voice mail systems record the time of your call.

Caveat: Some systems also list the extension it comes from. If your company has one of these, leave the message through your own voice mail box rather than calling the extension directly from outside of the company.

CASE STUDY

The "Doolittle" Sisters

In the first position I held following graduation (not including a worshipful stance in the dorm lavatory), I was a management trainee with a large insurance company in a New England city.

It was blissful in many ways. I had a lot of freedom. After work, I did not have to worry about work. (Not that I ever did work.) I could leave my job at work and spend my money freely.

In those days, the insurance business was practically a license to print money. Oh, we would pay off claims when we had to, but the investment of the premiums, which were higher than justifiable, produced income far above any claims.

But the best part of this job was three women in the Personnel Department. They were popularly known as the "Doolittle Sisters," because *they never did any work.*

Many people held this against them. Not I. I was inspired. They gave me the first conscious inklings of ineffectiveness as a way of life.

Personnel is an important but underappreciated department. It tends to be a dumping ground. But the Doolittle Sisters dumped right back.

Suppose you needed a medical form. You had better be nice to the Doolittle Sisters. Suppose you needed to review your personnel file. You had better be nice to the Doolittle Sisters. Suppose you wanted your raise processed in a timely manner, or your medical claim, or your tuition reimbursement, or your subscriptions, or you wanted your new-hire request dealt with responsibly. *You had better be nice to the Doolittle Sisters—and leave Superman's cape alone.*

A lot of people didn't approve of their power, but almost everybody kept their mouths shut. *They knew better.*

One didn't. He complained. I'll call him Hubert, although his name was Tom. Hubert, the nerdy company librarian, documented their abuse of power and made a stink. The eyes of senior management were drawn to the Doolittle Sisters. An investigation was begun.

This was the first time I saw the power of faking documentation after the fact. Hubert had truthfully complained that a claim for major dental repairs had been ignored by the Doolittle Sisters. He protested that he was being taken to court by his dentist *and* his oral surgeon. They were threatening to repossess his teeth, maybe even his mouth!

Well, the Doolittle Sisters processed the forms and backdated them successfully through their professional connections. They produced the "evidence" to the investigators. They were also able to "prove" that the check had been waiting for three months and that Hubert had ignored *repeated* calls to come pick it up. It was too large to send through the interoffice mail.

The beautiful part was yet to come. Hubert was undergoing therapy. And what therapy it was! I don't feel comfortable talking about his problem here, but let me say that he was a nut indeed. I guess it takes all kinds.

The Doolittle Sisters leaked the results of Hubert's psychological tests. Hubert cracked up—and now lives in a cardboard box near Ninety-second Street and Broadway in New York, where he practices his unique brand of performance art.

The Doolittle Sisters, however, have retired and gone their separate ways. One lives in Florida; one in Arizona, and one in Hawaii.

I think you get the picture.

There are many paths to ineffectiveness. Truly ineffective people generally do not attack others—unless they are *effective*. They prefer to aid and abet the ineffectiveness of others (although not very well).

You, as an ineffective person, will gradually learn new techniques of procrastination. But don't be in a hurry about it.

HABIT 3: DON'T WASTE TIME SETTING PRIORITIES

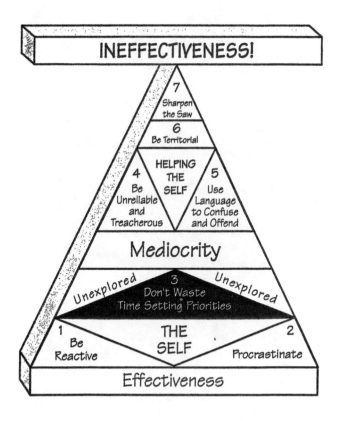

Avoid the Trap of
Effective Time Management

Time is dead as long as it is being clicked off by little wheels; only when the clock stops does time come to life.
—William Faulkner, *The Sound and the Fury*

We all hear about setting priorities. From childhood on, we're told "Hurry up!" and "Time is money," as if we needed to hear these things. At work, people commonly speak of the satisfaction of crossing items off of "to-do" lists. This is *not* my idea of satisfaction.

Don't get me wrong. Time *is* money. The less overall work you can do within a given amount of time, the better off you'll be. Your salary will not change, as you know, even if you can cram more work into a given amount of time. The real-life corollary to the infantile formulation "Time is money" is "Time is the *same* amount of money."

There are those who argue that working hard to get ahead can increase income, and I must grudgingly admit that this is true for a few. However, for most of us, advancement comes from being around long enough to get promoted or get hired by another company.

This fact begs the question, "How can I tolerate waiting around?" The answer is, "By being ineffective."

Life is strange. So often what seems reasonable is in fact unnecessary and tiresome. This insight is a bit of what is now known as "counterintuitive wisdom," and it applies to time management. If you use time carefully with an eye to productivity, you will find yourself doing too much and becoming exhausted, thus reducing leisure time on and off the job. *And you don't want that to happen.*

You want to be ineffective. When you're having fun, you don't pay attention to time. So, when you're being ineffective, don't obsess about time, or you will become more effective. This particular piece of counterintuitive wisdom will be second nature by the time you finish this book—or sooner, if you're really good at ineffectiveness.

As under the other habits, there are basic principles to use. This habit, however, finds its heart in the implementation. (Don't let that word scare you—if there were a more pleasant word available, I'd use it.) The tactics that follow are only the foundation of a concerted attack on effective time management. It is up to you to build walls, a roof, and other amenities. Once you have done that, you will be a terribly ineffective manager of time—and a happier person for it!

This diagram illustrates the "Circle of Deflection," a relative to the "Wall of Confusion." It is a great help in avoiding dealing with dreary, boring, work-related issues.

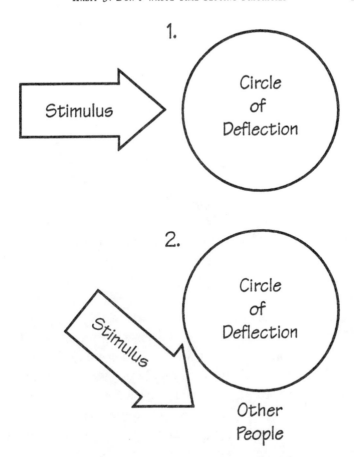

The four basic tactics I follow under this habit are:

- Float from problem to problem.
- Discard your to-do lists—daily.
- Don't update your Rolodex regularly.
- Use planners to decrease effectiveness while increasing the appearance of effectiveness.

These tactics will greatly increase your enjoyment of the time you are compelled to spend at work. They will serve you in good stead for as long as you pretend to work.

Float from problem to problem. This basic tactic is beautiful in its simplicity. Don't think of problems negatively. Think of them as flowers. Think of yourself as a butterfly enjoying a warm summer day. Float to a problem and alight. Scoop up some credit, as a butterfly scoops up pollen from a flower. Then float on.

The butterfly leaves the flower intact, if slightly altered. You leave the problem to someone else, *who may be slightly altered*. You and the butterfly are richer for truly meager efforts.

There are, however, several issues in the human world which simply don't arise in the insect world. Make sure these problems span your and the other people's areas of responsibility. If a problem is totally in your area of responsibility, refer to the principles outlined under Habit 1, particularly "When you screw up, require your subordinates to fix the problem. (Don't fix it yourself under *any* circumstances.)" and "Be vague, but demand precision."

The following illustration shows the intersection of circles of irresponsibility.

If the problem does cross boundaries, then float on over!

Ask some questions and write down—*or at least pretend to write down*—the answers. Contribute advice and solicit advice. Then put this in writing and send a memo to someone.

To whom you send this memo is important, but more important is to whom you send copies. These are the people

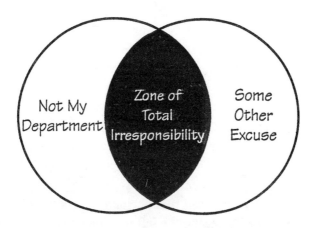

Circles of Irresponsibility

who will note that you're making an effort, however ineffective it may in reality be.

Now float away. If you've been really ineffective, reward yourself and come in late the next day—or two!

Discard your to-do lists—daily. I know what I wrote earlier about these despicable scratchings and the exaggerated—I mean invented—satisfaction of crossing items off them. What is actually satisfying, however, is discarding to-do lists! That's why I say, *Discard your to-do lists—daily.*

You can deal with those items that require only phone calls or that can be referred to, or (better yet), blamed on other departments. Don't transfer more than one or two items to the next day's to-do list. Items will gradually resolve themselves and disappear—or, as noted previously under Habit 1, you can later fake having taken care of them.

After your assistant and others have taken care of some of

the rest of the items, simply throw the list away. For a truly cathartic experience, *burn it!* Use the flames to light a cigarette. The psychic benefits are out of this world.

Don't update your Rolodex regularly. Only occasionally should new addresses and phone and fax numbers be added to your Rolodex; that is, when you have no choice because this person is going to crop up in your life regularly.

If you will need to call this person only occasionally, you will be better off keeping the information on scraps of paper or looking it up on old correspondence. That way, you will reply more slowly and thus *will not be the first name* to enter the person's mind when he or she is dealing with a problem that might relate to you.

By returning calls more slowly, you will increase your stature in their eyes. *You must be very busy!*

To top off these effective tactics of ineffectiveness, I must add a real classic: **Use planners to decrease effectiveness while increasing the appearance of effectiveness.** This is beautifully ineffective.

There are numerous "planners" and personal calendars on the market now. Their use gives the impression of serious-ness and organization. The eye sends impulses to the brain; the brain interprets and *sees.* If the eyes see a person writing down appointments, notes, and the like in a notebook with sheets of paper printed specifically to accommodate such items the brain will *see* organization and effectiveness.

Not only that, the planner will help you when you need to fake documentation. On top of that, you can "lose" your planner in a burglary, mugging, or car theft, or some other concocted tragedy, which need not be reported to the police—*just to your colleagues*. (Did you know that "gullible" is not in the dictionary?) Your whole life was in there!

This setback will buy you sympathy galore—and, even better, *excuses galore*. Because of the trauma, you will even be able to stay home from work for at least a day or two, giving you the best chance to catch up on daytime TV since the last time you called in sick.

The important thing to remember is *the misuse of the planner, not the type of planner*. Probably it is best to use the same kind each year, but even that is a minor consideration. Unfortunately, you'll have to familiarize yourself with the planner's elements, in order to misuse them properly. (For example, you may want to use the "reminder" sections when faking documentation.)

Another factor to consider is price. Some planners are not cheap. One way around this is to request one as a Christmas present. That way, you can brag about your planner and give the impression that it's very important to you—which it is, in a sense.

CASE STUDY

A Former Colleague, Now a Rival

A former employee of Minor Associates once called himself "Rain Man," and that's what I'll call him for this case study. I'm not going to tell you his real name because he is now a competitor, and a threateningly ineffective one at that, and I don't want to give him any help.

Rain Man gave himself his nickname, which he no longer

uses for professional reasons, in honor of the Dustin Hoffman character in the movie of the same name. It proved to be a brilliant disguise. However, unlike the cinematic Rain Man, he was hardly capable of counting to ten without losing interest, *especially* if work was involved. He was, however, a wealth of useless information on an amazing variety of topics.

Rain Man used to say some strange things and do some even stranger things, but, most of all, he *never wasted any time setting priorities*. He came in to the office almost every workday, it's true, but he did not make himself exceptionally useful. Since I am not particularly useful, I wondered if I should even keep him around.

But I did keep him around, and even gave him the usual inadequate, perfunctory raises. I admired his ineffectiveness and thought I could learn from him.

I was *wrong!* Rain Man was *learning from me!* (In fact, he is the inspiration for this book. If he could learn from me and take the lessons on the road, *without my making any money off it*, then maybe I should sell my wisdom more widely, in book form. I need the money and want it more than him.)

On a typical day, Rain Man would first be seen eating a hearty breakfast at the diner across the street at around ten or so in the morning. Once actually at work, Rain Man used to wander around the office, stopping in to visit friends, trading tips on the races and comparing lottery systems. (Rain Man's system was particularly ineffective in that sometimes he forgot to completely fill out the form).

He would, in time, go to his office and close the door and pretend to return important phone calls. Then he would open the door and work hard at his computer, perfecting his solitaire technique.

One of my favorite moments was when he interrupted a staff meeting to reveal the name of the two ridges that run from the bottom of the human nose to the upper lip. As it turns out, these can be very important in identifying people in old photographs.

All this time he was building relationships with *my clients!* I never gave him that much to do because it *was never done on time unless it didn't matter.*

And therein lies the rub. Rain Man never wasted time setting priorities. He just did what came naturally and used the tactics I describe in this chapter to sleaze by.

Now he's in business for himself.

I do admire him. But if you find out who he is and hire him, take my word for it—*you'll be sorry.*

Earlier I wrote that these tactics are just the foundation of avoiding the trap of effective time management. That said, they are a strong foundation. *Practice these principles, and you will not lack opportunities for fun and games without worrying about wasting time.*

Part Three
HELPING THE SELF

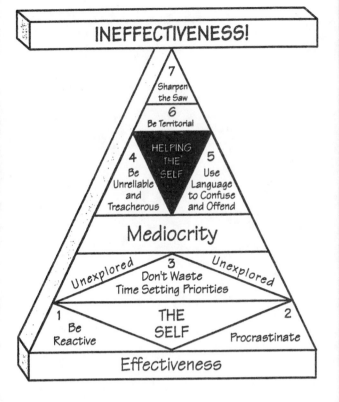

He who makes a beast of himself gets rid of the pain of being a man.
—SAMUEL JOHNSON

This part, encompassing Habits 4, 5, and 6, is entitled "Helping the Self." As with Part One, the title is apt. The theme of the next three habits is helping the self—*yourself*. You must help yourself because no one else is going to help you. This is a fact—deny it at your own risk. (Not that I'm worried. If you've made it this far, you're not into denial.)

The overall theme of these three habits is protectiveness, secretiveness, and self-aggrandizement. These traits are essential to safeguarding one's place in an organization.

Place. Let's examine that word. It means *a lot.* You've got to be aware of your place and its prerogatives. You've also got to make others aware of their place—especially those below you who might encroach on your position. As for those above you, they *will* make you aware of your place. They have to, they want to, and they like it. *You have to suck-up.*

The first issue is making others aware of *their* place. This is, for obvious reasons, more fun for most of us than being made aware of *our* place, although the ability to accept the depredations of ineffective people above you is essential.

Just remember that *someday you'll be there*. Then you can take revenge on those below you by virtue of the accidental order in which you were born.

By now, you already know the mechanics of making those below you aware of their lowly station. That's what the first three habits are all about. Now you need to learn the spirit of making them pay—and getting used to letting those above you make you pay (see below).

The second issue is dealing with your boss's reminding you of your place. There are two basic ways to deal with this. One is the art of the suck-up, which is profiled under Habit 4. The second is to support such concepts as teamwork, empowerment, and "boundarylessness," which many consultants *(but not I)* are forcing on corporations these days.

These ideas and policies can really increase the effectiveness of your organization, and are obviously all dangerous if applied to you. But you may be able to use them to great benefit against those above you on the totem pole.

The three habits in this section are:

4. Be unreliable and treacherous.
5. Use language to confuse and offend.
6. Be territorial.

These habits are complementary and symbiotic, which means they feed off each other. Together, they are a powerful force for ineffectiveness.

4. *Be unreliable and treacherous.* This is becoming a great American tradition—it's one of the things America's corporations and leaders do best. Never mind those "cherry tree" fables and "Honest Abe." That doesn't work any more. When it comes to this, we're a world leader. This habit goes right up there with "Nice guys finish last" and "Possession is nine-tenths of the law." I think human nature dictates it. In a spare four words, it lays out one of the basic principles of all social intercourse (in every sense of the word). *Ignore it at your own peril!* (I am confident that you will love it!)

5. *Use language to confuse and offend.* This is also becoming a great American tradition. It was practiced brilliantly by Ronald Reagan and his oh-so-ineffective-yet-successful sidekick, Lee Atwater. He got people elected by wide margins, and they went on to be reelected again and again—*without doing a damn thing worthwhile!* Today, Rush Limbaugh and Howard Stern are wonderful virtuosos of this habit.

To confuse and offend, you must avoid clarity yet push people's buttons rudely and gleefully. Both of these ploys, which are essential to ineffectiveness, greatly increase the space for ineffective behavior.

I'm ineffective; you should be, too.

6. *Be territorial*. This is second nature to man and beast alike, but we are so often admonished—*from an early age*—to "share and share alike." My advice: *Don't!* Territory, guarded by whatever means are available, *and however worthless it may be*, is the historical basis of wealth, or at least an income.

In a modern corporation, this is more true than ever. You must be ready to repulse attackers and, if possible, annex others' territories. If you're really, really good at ineffectiveness, you'll take it all over. *That's called "making it to the top."*

HABIT 4: BE UNRELIABLE AND TREACHEROUS

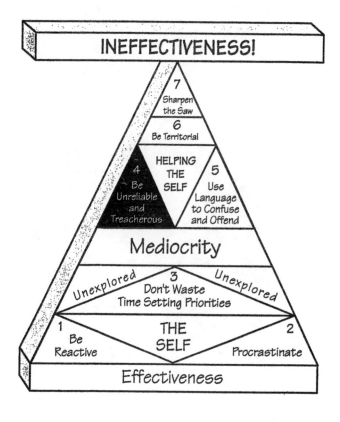

ADVANCE YOUR
AGENDA SHAMELESSLY

QUESTION: *What is a Hollywood friend?*
ANSWER: *Someone who stabs you in the front.*

We're all out for something, even if that something is humiliation and rejection (which are *not* ineffective goals). What ineffective people want is income and advancement without having to work for it. Money is sweet. Without having worked for it, money is sweeter—*much sweeter.*

Part of ineffectiveness is the advancement of your agenda, which must be two-pronged. One prong is income; the other is workload. They should move in opposite directions—*specific* opposite directions. Income must increase *as* workload decreases.

If income and workload increase in tandem, you're doing something wrong—*very* wrong. (If income and workload decrease in tandem, you're probably unemployed.) Go back to the beginning of the book and, hanging your sadly *effective* head in shame, get in touch with your *inner ineffective child*.

This illustration lays out this basic and simple goal.

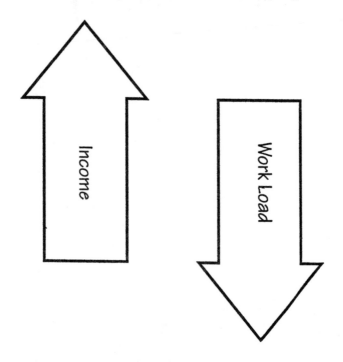

The Path to True Success

Any corporation has conflicts—personal, professional, and logical. The secret to advancing one's agenda of more money with less work is to exploit these conflicts. Reduced to its simplest form, which is certainly good enough for the likes of us, the idea is to position oneself away from conflicts between figures more powerful than yourself and avoid explicitly taking sides or getting involved in these sordid and ultimately stupid battles.

You *do* want to be informed and, quietly, help both sides out in those areas related to their specific areas of control. *But don't help either out against the other* (not that your help would be wanted, needed, or even very useful). This will make these folks look kindly on you, even as they stab each other in the back.

Once you have set up this situation, which is similar to suspended animation (the best of all worlds) or armed neutrality (which, like Switzerland, implies too much work), you will be ready to practice the four fundamental skills of looking out for number one:

- The art of being a protégé to more than one person.
- The art of the suck-up.
- The art of the backstab.
- The art of avoiding mentoring.

These skills will serve you well in your continuing epic quest to sleaze your way to a comfortably ineffective niche.

The art of being a protégé to more than one person. In today's rapidly changing economy, being a protégé to one person is not enough. You must pretend to learn from and respect two or more people higher than you in the corporate structure.

That's not as hard as it sounds. In today's unstable and pathological business environment, *everyone is looking for someone to feel better than.* You can easily fill this role for several people.

The beauty of this approach is twofold: it gives you more chances to advance your agenda, and it makes you harder to fire. If things go wrong with one mentor, you've still got others who will defend you against *their* enemy's depredations.

Of course, the joke's not on you!

The art of the suck-up. In order to be a protégé to two or more corporate you-know-whats, you must master the art—and it is an *art*—of sucking up. Fundamentally, this involves the simple realization that *your livelihood depends on someone else.*

Look around you. Is your apartment or home comfortable? Do you have a home entertainment center? Do you owe big bucks on credit cards you have irresponsibly maxed out? If so, you better understand the necessity of sucking up.

But how to suck up? First of all, what does the phrase imply? It's graphic. I think you get the picture.

The problem is to translate the graphic allegory into practices that can be carried out during normal working hours in full view of your colleagues.

Quite simply, you must heap praise on higher-ups, *whether they deserve it or not.* In fact, to do a really good job, the whole notion of praise being "deserved" or "earned" must be erased from your mind.

I'm reminded of what an Eastern European writer, whose long name I've forgotten and whose books I never read, said about "socialist realism," which was the approved literary style under communism. He said it was "writing in praise of the authorities so that even they can understand."

Sucking up is "capitalist realism."

Praise anything and everything done by those to whom you must suck up—*then praise some more.* Suggest meetings, then refer favorably to others' ideas and work during these meetings. Ask for advice, then praise the advice. Some suggested suck-ups are listed below:

STANDARD SUCK-UPS

- "That's exactly what I was looking for."
- "Thank you for your wisdom and insight."
- "You just put into words the idea I had but couldn't quite put my finger on."
- "That's a great suit."
- "Very funny." [Follow this remark with realistic-sounding laughter—think about something which really *is* funny if it helps.]
- "I loved the way you handled _____ ."
- "As you brilliantly said, _____ ."
- "You're an amazing genius."
- "I'm not worthy."

As your ineffectiveness grows, you will think of more and more standard suck-ups and develop your own personal style of sucking up. In this way, you will protect and advance your place in what I call the "corporate sucking-up order."

The art of the backstab. This skill is important when you're looking to advance to a new position and increased level of ineffectiveness. Undoubtedly, there will be more than one possible candidate for this position. Worse, one or more of these candidates will probably—in fact, *almost* *certainly*—be better than you! (Even worse is if one or more of these candidates is more ineffective than you. Then you *really* have to watch out.)

Before you can backstab your colleagues, you must become a trusted team member. Otherwise, no one will believe you. I list some standard methods of backstabbing below.

STANDARD BACKSTABBING METHODS

- Spreading malicious and untrue gossip (all rumors are assumed to be true).
- Delaying important documents.
- Giving bad advice off the record, then publicizing the resulting disasters.
- Tipping people off to spurious job openings and then reporting that _____ is looking for a new job.
- Damning with faint praise.
- Symphathizing with the personal problems of others. ("What a shame that _____ can't stop drinking and snorting cocaine. He/she could be so good.")

As in the art of the suck-up, these are just suggested *starting points*. If you want to read further on this subject, study British gentry and royalty or develop an interest in the politics of the Arab world.

The art of avoiding mentoring. I've already gone into detail about how to exploit subordinates, which is a very good beginning to avoiding mentoring. The fact is, however, that as you advance your agenda, people will notice your progress. This is unavoidable, however invisible you may think you are. (We already know that you're transparent.)

What you don't want, however, is for someone to latch on to you and practice the time-honored principles outlined in this book—*against you!*

The first thing to do is to make life miserable for your subordinates. As noted earlier, this both gives you designated scapegoats and preemptively removes threats. I'm not going to repeat the principles noted earlier, since they should be second nature by now.

I will, however, add a couple of powerful tools of oppression. The first is *the assignment of impossible tasks.* The second is *the assignment of possible tasks with impossibly short deadlines.* Both of these, especially if heaped on, will reduce anyone to a mass of quivering jelly.

The one exception to these principles is if someone to whom you suck up assigns one of their lower (than you) protégés to you. Now you've got a problem. What to do?

Quite simply, *suck down.* After a suitable but short (as short as possible) period of time, recommend this person for a new job—a job *as far away from you as possible.* Perhaps you will even be able to recommend this person for the job of someone you, and maybe others, are backstabbing!

CASE STUDY

A Movie Producer

This story is an uplifting piece of wonder if I ever heard one.

This producer, a close friend as well as a consulting client, has climbed the ladder of the movie business—without ever having a real success that he actually can truly claim credit for.

That is not to say that *he has not claimed credit—and gotten it.*

Let me start by telling you how he handled a recent phone call from a writer. The producer, whom I shall call Slim, because there is so little *really* there, commissioned a script from a talented young writer, whom I shall call Art.

Not that Slim intended to make the movie. He needed some ideas for another movie—any other movie.

I was in Slim's office, enjoying his stimulating company and his stimulants, when Art called. Art was *smart*. This was proven by the fact that he had gotten through to Slim.

Slim decided to reveal his technique to me, and to sound far-off and important, so he switched the call to the speaker phone.

Art asked how Slim was doing, and engaged in some other pleasantries. These were a real waste of time. Slim is not a pleasant person. Pleasantries are wasted on such people.

Art then asked what Slim thought of the script. Slim's reply was brilliant. If Einstein had devoted his intellect to ineffectiveness, he could not have come up with this:

"I don't know. I'm the only one who's read it so far."

Art was silent for a long period of time. So were Slim and I, although eventually I had to run out of the office before I burst into laughter.

After Slim refused to ever give a real answer or pay the tiny option sum, Art complained to his agent, who was not one of the top agents on the Coast. Art was not yet ready for them, and they were not ready for him.

Art tried back again and again, while Slim "developed" new scripts, many of which incorporated ideas that an impartial observer could have seen in Art's screenplay. Ideas, however, unlike plots, are not protected by copyright. (At least I think that's true.)

As Art complained, Slim began spreading the word: "Art _____ is a difficult writer. He is making *crazy* claims against me."

Art's agent fired him. He wasn't bringing in any commissions. Art's next agent was not only a sleaze, he was stupid and had no connections. This agent and Art both soon went broke.

Art now lives in a derelict building on the Lower East Side, "Loisaida," of Manhattan. He sells ratty poetry and begs for a living, and has a wicked heroin habit.

Slim lives in an eighteen-bedroom mansion in Bel Air.

━━

It is human to desire. Zen Buddhism may advocate liberating oneself from desire, but I advocate getting used to it and satisfying it. Translate desire into a strategy of advancement without performance, of increasing income and perks while decreasing work. This will liberate you from drudgery, but not desire. Ineffectiveness is a powerful seducer.

HABIT 5: USE LANGAUGE TO CONFUSE AND OFFEND

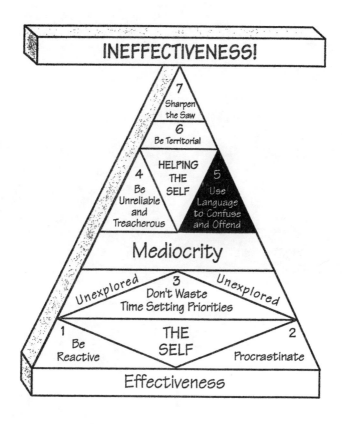

AVOID CLARITY,
BUT PUSH PEOPLE'S BUTTONS

SUE ANN NIVENS: Mary, what do you think turns on a man?

MARY RICHARDS (*exasperated*): Sue Ann, I haven't the slightest idea.

SUE ANN: I know that. I was just trying to make your day.

—*The Mary Tyler Moore Show*

The wonderful thing about people is the fact that we can *speak*. We communicate—*with language!* It's the basis of civilization, such as it is. And, more important, it's the basis of ineffectiveness. Without civilization, there could be no ineffectiveness. And without ineffectiveness, why have civilization? Without ineffectiveness, there would be no reason to maintain civilization.

(Have you even seen an ineffective wild animal? They couldn't survive, even in herds—but there are ineffective domesticated animals. Domesticated turkeys, for example, drown in rainstorms because they look upward and open their mouths. By roasting and eating them, we're doing them a favor.)

But why speak? (Is autism ineffective? It's hard to tell, but it doesn't appear to be particularly effective.) You speak to further your goals. The human race developed speech in order to further its goals—comfort and control. You, as a human being, can, should, and *must* do the same.

We've all heard a lot about grammar, clarity, and the like, but are these the ends ineffective people should pursue? If, as I passionately believe, we are living in an age of increasing ineffectiveness, there is hope to be taken from the declining standards of discourse in America.

Take all those lessons about such trivialities as "who" versus "whom," pronoun/antecedent agreement, clear, plain speech, descriptive, lively verbs, and the like, and *throw them out the window*—if you haven't already. (*Note:* If portions of this book seem dangerously clear, take heart. It's for a good cause.)

The diagram on the next page shows the effect of confusing and offensive language on a previously centered, competent, and even effective person.

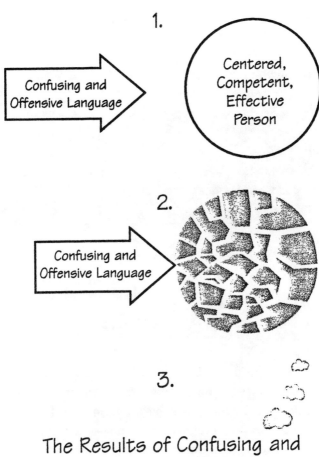

The Results of Confusing and Offensive Language

So how should the ineffective person take advantage of humanity's language ability? In my career as an ineffective executive and now as an ineffective consultant, I have found six fundamental principles of ineffective, unclear, or indeed offensively thoughtless communication:

- State the obvious.
- Pretend to care.
- Emphasize points unnecessarily (thus question-ing someone's intelligence).
- Furrow your brow with a mixture of concern, pity, and malevolence (especially when dealing with subordinates).
- Master the backhanded insult.
- Recap what has just been said, trivializing it in the process.

If you can put these into practice in true ineffective fashion, you will blaze a path through the corporate world that will make the Great Chicago Fire look like a Cub Scout campfire.

State the obvious. This tactic has been pursued for centuries by lawyers, politicians, and, more recently, scientists. Lately, even comedians have gotten into the act.

The best way to do this is to remark significantly on something everyone knows so well that it seldom penetrates their consciousness. That doesn't mean that they don't think about it. Thinking occurs on many levels in the mind. *Original thinking often occurs subconsciously, where it should remain.*

Short-circuit this process. Bring these commonplace ver-ities to the surface. Remark on schedules, avoidance of typos, getting addressed right, and the like. Since thinking occurs on many levels, if you disturb this process by stating the obvious, you will set everyone else back—making you look better!

One added benefit: By stating those obvious things most people justifiably if unconsciously ignore, you will call attention to your own intellect—without even really thinking! This is truly the best of all possible worlds.

Pretend to care. The importance of pretense is second to none. (Remember the great Hollywood saying: "The key is sincerity. Once you can fake that, you've got it made.") Fortunately, most of us grow up learning how to fake concern. Pretense is part and parcel of life.

Most of us know the usual forms of pretending to care: false smiles, meaningless compliments, ostensibly con-

WAYS TO PRETEND TO CARE

- Note colleagues' birthdays, birthdays of their offspring and relatives, their anniversaries, and the like. Then *wait until at least one week after the occasion* to wish then a "belated" whatever it was.
- Pry into personal problems and then offer "thoughtful, heartfelt" and thoroughly condescending and contemptible advice. (Be sure to save the revelations gained thereby for gossip later.)
- Give false congratulations on successes and promotions. *Really make these over-the-top; pride goeth before a fall.*
- Express sympathy to colleague in a tough spot, then let his/her boss know that he/she is complaining.

cerned eye contact, etc. What I can offer here are more sophisticated forms of pretense and faking concern. The list on the previous page covers some of the best of these.

Emphasise points unnecessarily (thus questioning someone's intelligence). These can range from the trivial to the banal. But no matter what, they *must* be common-sense. For example, in a memo, if you think that the subject under consideration—say, a photo of a new building in a brochure—should in some fashion be big, type the word "big" in all capital letters, perhaps even in boldface as well: "**BIG.**"

If you think a contractual point is important, really emphasize its importance by setting it apart, underlining words, and maybe even pulling points out and putting them in a box—*even* if everyone else agrees. Actually, *especially if everyone else agrees.*

Furrow your brow with a mixture of concern, pity, and malevolence (especially when dealing with subordinates). What I mean by this is that body language is a very important part of all ineffective persons' arsenals. This particular gesture is the corporate version of what "wise guys" call "the look." Al Capone used to have a grand old time intimidating victims with cold-blooded stares, which he used to practice in front of the mirror. Many present-day organized-crime figures still do this, especially in Brooklyn.

In corporate America, however, it is considered bad form to look at colleagues as if you literally want to kill them. But you can look at them in this intimidating manner, which suggests that *you know something they don't*. It indicates a combination of dismay and disappointment. This can be used on people whose jobs are shakier than yours, if they are below you on the corporate sucking-up order, and especially if they're *dependent* on you. The look of fright that a good furrowed brow can induce in a subordinate will light up an otherwise all-too-effective day.

Master the backhanded insult. This is truly a sinful pleasure. Combined with the furrowed brow, you can really shake people up with this one. To refresh your memory, such as it is, a good backhanded insult must always degrade while pretending to compliment or at least console. I list some examples below.

SUGGESTED BACKHANDED INSULTS

• "Very good. You're getting much better."
• "That's a very interesting idea. If only it could work."
• "It's great how polyester is coming back into fashion. You look wonderful!"
• "Go home now. You've tried very hard and need some rest." (This comes after a frustrating and ultimately unsuccessful effort).
• "Are you okay? Normally you look so healthy."

Any my personal favorite:

• "I like you. I don't know what's wrong with everybody else."

Recap what has already been said, trivializing it in the process. Recapping what has already been said is wonderfully time-wasting, not to mention *totally* unnecessary. Since the point of Habit 5 is to avoid clarity and push people's buttons, reduce the importance of key points while recapping. In other words, take out elements of insight while seeming to do the point(s) justice.

Fortunately, this is easier than it sounds. For example, you can downgrade words. Substitute "crystal ball gazing" for "trend forecasting" and "seeking the lowest common denominator" for "market research." Another method is to omit subtle distinctions. This is especially annoying and trivializing. The person whose work you are recapping in a trivial fashion will probably become defensive or at least try to elaborate on your distorted recap.

This response will only play right into your hands.

CASE STUDY

The Politics of Ineffectiveness

To illustrate the power of using language to confuse and offend and to show the tremendous ineffectiveness that comes from this approach, I think we should turn to the world of politics.

There is no area of public discourse where more confusion has been sown. And, as I noted much earlier, while the ineffectiveness at the highest levels of government is probably beyond the reach of the large majority of readers of this book, it is truly *inspirational*.

I have been an admirer of "hot button" politics for a long time. The best way to use language to confuse and offend is to push people's buttons.

Think of it this way. If you're running the campaign of an ineffective politician, or merely providing high-priced advice (as I prefer), you've got some distinct problems. He/she got elected, all right, but as the voters look around them as they go about their lives, they're bound to notice that the government is functioning poorly—or not at all.

Of course, this is the point of ineffective politics and government. The problem is that taxes take a big bite out of people's paychecks—and their lives—and from time to time the voters *will expect things to get done*.

This quaint hope must, of course, be resisted. There are several tactics which deflect attention from the ineffective incumbent's lousy record and cast doubt on the opponent's worthiness to hold office and represent his or her constituency.

The wonderful thing about these tactics is that they make the electorate cynical about the entire process—and less likely to bother to vote anyway. As political ineffectiveness has increased, voter turnout has decreased. It's what some call a vicious circle, but I call it the *ineffective feedback loop*.

First of all, let us give thanks for the thirty second political television commercial. While you can be meaningful, accurate, and even just plain honest in thirty seconds, it is so much easier to be meaningless, inaccurate, and just plain dishonest. This will offend a few (who may or may not vote), but it will confuse a lot more—especially as cynicism increases and voter interest decreases.

Now let's examine the "sound bite." These seven- to ten-second sentences or phrases, specifically scripted into politicians' speeches by soundbite specialists for the evening news, are *absolutely useless* for the communication of ideas. But the television-shortened attention span of much of the public demands them. They also allow news show producers much more leeway in pacing broadcasts and scheduling commercials—and they increase ratings.

They are also, not so incidentally, perfect for pushing buttons, which is about all they can do. A button is an area of irrational sensitivity. To push it, be *quick and dirty*.

The coup de grace of all ineffective campaigning is, of course, "going negative." Polls show that, overall, voters dislike negative campaigning. Polls also show that, overall, voters want the issues addressed substantively. But if you go negative, *you're going to take some voters with you.* You're also going to lower the tone of the race. Your opponent will have no choice but to match you, insult for insult, distortion for distortion.

Ineffective politicians, by negative campaigning, can always swing a few voters their way—*and turn off a larger number of voters entirely.* This is, of course, entirely to the benefit of ineffective politicians and ineffective government.

You gotta love it.

As noted above, speech is the basis of civilization, which is, in turn, the basis for ineffectiveness. So practice those backhanded insults and hone your insincerity! Implicitly question your colleagues' intelligence and judgment, even as you maintain a facade of cooperation. *You have nothing to lose but work other people should be doing for you.*

HABIT 6: BE TERRITORIAL

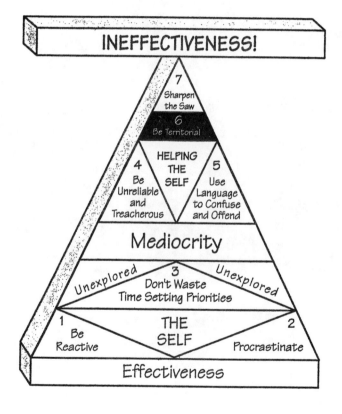

GUARD YOUR TURF, HOWEVER WORTHLESS IT MAY BE

You would make a fine manager. You're sneakier than I thought.
—CONGRESSMAN MORLEY, *THE FARMER'S DAUGHTER*

As I brilliantly noted previously, in an organization, position is paramount. Position is defined by what you control, or what you theoretically are at least supposed to oversee. This fiefdom is commonly known as your "turf." To a large extent, its size and importance determine the size and importance of your paycheck.

No matter how worthless it may seem or *in fact really is*, you must defend your turf at all costs. Even a contemptible position with severely limited authority is preferable to unemployment. And such contemptible positions are often the sad and unjust treatment that ineffective people often must put up with.

I have found five basic practices key to guarding your turf. They are useful no matter what that turf may be. To wit (so to speak):

> • Delegate responsibility but not power.
> • Involve yourself in the corporate game of mutual back-scratching.
> • Steal ideas.
> • Hire the ineffective and promote them away from you.
> • Pull rank when reason fails, as it surely must for all truly ineffective people.

As usual, let's take a closer look:

Delegate responsibility but not power. This is truly one of the great practices underlying the successful protection of turf. It is also supremely ineffective.

What you do is you give an underling the *responsibility* for a particular task or a continuing function of the organization, but you do not put him/her in a position to carry out the actions necessary for this task. For that, he/she must come to you.

This puts your victim in an unusually dependent position. You can delay taking care of the requests. You can nitpick the work. You can set impossible deadlines. No one can complain, or you will really make life unpleasant.

By doing this, you get the work done without doing any work. You give the impression of doing work and can *totally control* your boss's perception of what's going on.

Finally, you keep these tasks within your area of responsibility, your *turf*, without lifting a finger!

Tell me that's not the way to work.

Involve yourself in the corporate game of mutual back-scratching. This is both important and fun, and it doesn't even hurt your visibility—or invisibility—or make you unnecessarily and dangerously articulate. Simply get involved in projects where a person or team is receiving contradictory signals. Then, cloaking yourself in the spirit of teamwork, start offering advice which sucks.

Continue your campaign by getting your name on the distribution list(s). *Put yourself in the loop.* Then give inane, screwy, half-baked advice—and demand to see how your wisdom is implemented. Offer constructive criticism coupled with implied dismay. Show up unexpectedly at the offices of people you are tormenting, then smile broadly, with obvious insincerity.

This behavior will accomplish nothing except improve your status and importance within the company—which is a lot!

Steal ideas. This is absolutely vital to successful ineffectiveness. Since you can't think of ideas on your own, you are left wondering how to get them. *Steal them!*

This is easiest to do to your subordinates. Simply encourage them to think for themselves and make suggestions. Then take these ideas, modify them slightly, and change a few of the terms. At the same time, tell the originator of the idea either (1) you're thinking about it, or (2) it will not work because of *whatever crappy excuse you happen to dream up.* (*Note:* If you used excuse number one, you will have to eventually follow up with excuse number two—I hope *before* you formally steal the idea. Excuse number one is simply a delaying tactic.

Other, "equal" colleagues are also good for stealing from, but this is potentially problematic. If they get on to your game, it can be trouble. You may have to backstab them, which you should never do unless it advances your career.

If backstabbing is merely a defensive maneuver due to a problem that you have initiated, it is a waste of time and energy that could better be devoted to leisure pursuits.

But if you can successfully steal from your colleagues, you will love yourself for it.

One very good place to steal from is the competition, but unfortunately, this is actually effective. Stealing from the competition is justifiable, however, if you use the stature you gain from it to be ineffective in other areas of your job.

Techniques can range from simply keeping your eyes open to what they're doing to such practices as industrial espionage and blackmail. I can't offer much advice on those tactics here (my lawyer advises that I keep my mouth shut), but I can say that stealing ideas from the competition will not only give you ideas, it can also garner you respect from the company for your fighting instincts.

Or you can pretend to have thought of the idea yourself. Take this tack if you haven't stolen any ideas lately that you've taken personal credit for.

Hire the ineffective and promote them away *from you.* This practice will help you develop ineffective allies within the company, a key help in both advancement and asscovering. *"I'll sort of scratch your back if you sort of scratch my back."*

In addition, by hiring the ineffective, you will avoid the threat that the effective can pose, especially in these dangerous times for the ineffective. *But beware:* As your ineffective subordinates develop their skills by observing you, they will themselves gradually become potential threats, or at least nuisances.

Solve this problem and gain allies by promoting them away from you. Deliver warm, indeed over-the-top, recommendations for them, which need not have *anything to do with the truth.* That way, they'll become somebody else's problem—*and the cycle can begin anew.*

Pull rank when reason fails, as it surely must for all truly ineffective people. This is the ground floor to guarding your turf. In fact, rank *determines* turf. For example, if a direct subordinate has a legitimate suggestion regarding procedures, work priorities, or the like, squash it flat. *You're* the boss, and you know better. That's *why* you're the boss. This blatantly untrue idea is the foundation of all corporate structures. Use it or lose it.

CASE STUDY

A Restaurant Manager Protects Her Turf

Let me tell you a story about the advantages of turf. A close friend and colleague, whom I have advised in the past on a professional basis, was the manager of a passable French restaurant with an inflated reputation, high prices, and a good expense-account business at both lunch and dinner. In other words, a lovely place for an ineffective.

My friend, whom I shall call Tabitha, although her name is Georgia, loves strawberries. *She loves strawberries.* Tabitha can't eat enough of them.

One day she hit upon a wonderful idea. Why not set up a contest for the best strawberries, among various suppliers in the city? This would mean pleasure for her and perhaps even good publicity for the restaurant.

She ordered her food buyer to organize the contest. After all, the food buyer was the one with the experience. This contest was, in fact, a great opportunity for the buyer, whom I shall call Cassandra. Tabitha realized in a glow of self-satisfaction that it was truly generous of her to delegate this duty to her food buyer, who was, at this time, still only "getting better" at her job.

But, just to have a little more fun, our manager/heroine backdated the memo a couple of days and hid it in a place the food buyer would not look for a couple more days—but *it was not so hidden as to be obviously concealed*. She also added the proviso that the participating suppliers had to provide their samples *for free*. After all, the publicity they would receive would pay for the strawberries many times over.

Cassandra began to despair. This did not particularly worry Tabitha. In fact, it was a source of mirth. (The ineffective never show pity except when they're pretending to care, as noted under Habit 5.) Viewed realistically, why should any supplier—there were, after all, only a handful of wholesalers—care to participate, *for free*, in such a contest? They stood to gain nothing but lost sales.

Cassandra began to receive regrets from suppliers who had been invited to participate in the strawberry contest, but Tabitha would hear nothing of it. She demanded that

Cassandra go back and try again. This resulted in anger and threats from the suppliers, a rough-and-tumble lot.

The contest collapsed before it got going. The restaurant had to run retractions of its ads trumpeting "this sea of strawberries, this surfeit of sweetness, this cornucopia of corn syrup."

The owner called Cassandra into his largely unused office, where Tabitha sat, holding back a wickedly amused grin. The owner, a Mr. Merde, summarily fired his once-promising food buyer. Many had held the position, but *none had survived.*

For Tabitha, the benefits were manifold. She destroyed a rival. She asserted her authority. She had a scapegoat for her own screw-ups. She won.

She protected her turf.

By now, you're well on your way to true ineffectiveness. But now it's time for the final habit, which allows you to become ever more ineffective. After taking a nice long break, read on!

Part Four
REPETITION

My old pappy used to say, "Son, hard work never hurt anyone—who didn't do it."
—BART MAVERICK, *Maverick*

This part is titled "Repetition," and with good reason. Its subject is *repetition*—the soul of all learning, even ineffective learning. (Face it: Learning is what you're doing by reading this book, however unpleasant "learning" may be.)

Babies learn to speak by imitating adults and then *repeating* this imitation until they get it right. By the same token, ineffective people "learn" from other ineffective people. You see ineffectiveness in action, you like it, and you want to be that way. You jump, or slide, right in, and embellish and expand your act by repetition and, alas, learning from experience. At least it's not hard to imitate ineffectiveness.

What you must seek is continuous improvement in ineffectiveness. After you read this book *to the end* (my sincere apologies), you will be able to deflect responsibility better, and you will be well on your way to undeserved success in your chosen calling—*without trying at all.* By the time you finish this book, you will be practicing ineffectiveness with ever increasing ineffectiveness, even arrogance. You will be failing upward all the time.

There is only one habit in this section. It is:

> 7. Sharpen the saw.

You may wonder what I mean by this. (Or you may not, or you may *not even care.*) Very simply, I mean that *you must continually sharpen your ineffective skills and tactics.* The higher you fail upward, the greater the stakes and the more onerous the demands—especially in this era of increasing lip service being paid to performance standards.

Think of a handsaw cutting through wood. Now think of a power saw. Probably when you began this book, you were as effective at cutting through the corporate structure as a handsaw is through hardwood. When you have finished this book and absorbed its contents, you will be like a power saw cutting through balsa wood.

HABIT 7: SHARPEN THE SAW

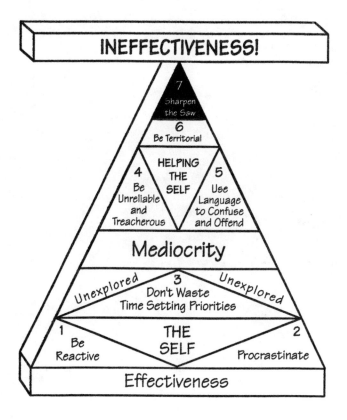

PRACTICE INEFFECTIVENESS WITH EVER-INCREASING CONFIDENCE, EVEN ARROGANCE

It takes a smart man to know he's stupid.
—BARNEY RUBBLE, *The Flintstones*

By now, if I've done my job, such as it is, you will be slouching toward the *conscious, premeditated practice of ineffectiveness*. You now have an ineffective mind and need only one more ingredient—the undying urge to remain ineffective, to resist organization, self-improvement, responsibility, and commitment.

I call this the "Downward Spiral of Ineffectiveness," as shown on the next page.

Under Habit 7, I offer four methods not only for remaining ineffective but also for becoming *even more ineffective.* One is quite specific, while the other three are more general: Let's take a look:

Use mistakes to advance your career. This is a tricky strategy, but very good if you can pull it off. (*Note:* I realize

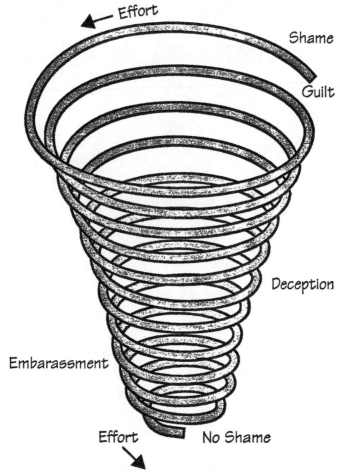

The Downward Spiral of Ineffectiveness

that this approach contradicts one of the rules I developed briefly under Habit 1, namely "When you screw up, require your subordinates to fix it. (Don't fix it yourself under *any* circumstances.)"

> • Use mistakes to advance your career.
> • Use being a party animal to advance you career.
> • Use pitiful behavior to advance you career.
> • Pretend to quit smoking and become an anti-
>   tobacco militant—or invert the process and
>   become a tobacco company executive.

Let me explain. I don't mean that you should admit *all* of your mistakes or even very many of them. That would be both suicidal and honest. Just a few mistakes, *carefully chosen*, and then properly acknowledged, can be employed to improve your standing in the company.

Remember the old saying your parents used to bore you with: "The only way to learn is by making mistakes." This is actually true to a very real extent, but the acquisition of real knowledge is not a subject we're concerned with here.

I know that corporations generally will use your mistakes against you. Hence the incredible amount of ass-covering, itself a great boon to ineffectiveness. But sometimes pretending to learn can score you points. This is especially true with the new emphasis on candor and honesty in business.

If you have properly developed two or more mentors, as discussed under Habit 5, you will be able to use this technique to surprisingly good effect.

Once in a while, *once in a great while*, admit a mistake openly. Even call attention to it. But do so only under the pretense that *you have "learned" from the mistake and will do better next time.*

Do this with an *air* of humble honesty and straightforward realism. (Note that I do not advocate *actual* humble honesty or straightforward realism.) Point out the minimal detriments, maybe even *benefits*, of your screwup, which you have learned from and which *others might well learn from, too*. You will be better off for it, although your colleagues will not.

Use being a party animal to advance your career. This is both tons of fun and a surprisingly powerful form of ineffectiveness. In this age of incest survivorship, codependency, twelve-step programs, self-pity, blame, positive affirmations, and other forms of navel contemplation, merrymaking (drinking) stands out as the ancient, time-honored method of avoidance—especially if you really don't party that much! (More on that later.)

Once you have established your position and set up your lines of miscommunication and distrust throughout the company, begin to party heavily. Use your expense account to take your colleagues out on the town for evenings of drunken debauchery. Come in late, bleary-eyed, and stumble through the day, smiling sickly.

If you can stand it, then come in early the following day and *look really busy*. Keep this up for as long as possible, then go in to see your boss and announce that you've attended your first AA meeting and will soon be going away for rehab for at least six weeks—*on the company health plan*.

When you return, you will be renewed!

The psychic benefits of partying heartily are probably second nature to you. Party animals are happy, smiling, fun people. I've never gotten sick of alcohol, and I seldom get sick from it anymore. Now, however, you will receive the benefits of the *perception of courage, responsibility, and honesty* as you confront your disease, which is nothing to be ashamed of.

Since you are established in the company and well liked by your coterie, who owe you some great nights on the town that they don't remember, you will be respected and admired for your forthright admission of your problem and your determination to start a new life.

This perception will have a powerful effect on your career path. (*Remember:* Perception and reality are two very different things.)

Before taking this step, surreptitiously check out your health plan's benefits for alcohol and drug rehab. (*Note:* Drug addiction, while often quite enjoyable, is not an advisable problem to develop. Drugs are *still* frowned upon at most companies, except perhaps in the record business.)

Then, if possible, pick out a rehab center in a place with beautiful scenery and a warm, sunny climate. (It is especially important, if you live in the Northern tier of states, to time your rehab for the winter months. "Face up to reality" *in Florida* in February! If you can't do this, at least *maximize* your time off.)

When you do finally return to work, be on time for the first day or two. Soak up the respect and goodwill. In a year, get a new, better, higher-paying job, and *start the process over again*.

Use pitiful behavior to advance your career.

Basically, this technique involves making people like you and then feel sorry for you. *Manipulate their emotions*, in other words.

I've covered many specific aspects of this practice, ranging from the art of the suck-up, to the judicious use of mistakes as career enhancers, to the ever popular manipulation of perceptions. All of these can fall under the heading of pitiful behavior.

In some cases, however, you will have to be a little more plain about your pathetic little self. Create sympathy for yourself by *debasing yourself.* (If you get off on this, *don't be ashamed.*)

Point out, obliquely, that you're overworked. You don't have enough help, but you know that *there's nothing anyone can do about it.* You don't get proper support from your subordinates. Your spouse/partner, whom you *still love,* isn't treating you right. You *used to smile.* You *used to laugh.* Now worry—*caused by others*—is eating your soul.

Don't be afraid to act harried or stressed when using this tactic. Just be sure you *always accurately gauge your audience's reaction and adjust your act accordingly.*

If it works, play it to the hilt. If it doesn't, move on to a new ploy. Whatever you do, don't even think about becoming effective just because you're debasing yourself. Get used to it.

Pretend to quit smoking and become an anti–tobacco militant—or invert this strategy and become a tobacco company executive. It's no secret that there a lot of angry people in America today. With good reason, a lot of us—and *I mean a lot of us*—are getting royally screwed. Of course, ineffective people like me are doing most of it.

So take advantage!

We have corporations which abuse power. We have criminals in our cities, our suburbs, and in our government. We have neighbors who complain when we play music too loud.

So what are millions of Americans protesting against? *Tobacco smoking!*

Plenty of people who can't stand tobacco smoked once and had no problem with it.

Not too long ago, I sat down in a restaurant with a friend, whom I'll call Bob. Before long, and, what really annoyed me, before we had even ordered drinks (this place has great martinis), Bob asked the waiter to be move us *further* into the nonsmoking section.

I decided not to ask him if he wanted to go outside and share a cigarette with me and instead mentioned that I had recently quit smoking. "Never have I felt better!" I assured him.

Bob is neither effective nor ineffective, which may be why I like him. He is not threatening, but he is a window into the lives of all those mediocre people out there. He has ineffective potential, but he doesn't work at or even think about it. Maybe this book will open Bob's eyes, or at least maybe I'll get royalties when he buys it. *(He ain't getting a free copy.)*

Upon hearing of my conversion to the nonsmoking blessed ones, Bob became exceedingly excited. He praised me to no end. In fact, I wish I had had a hidden tape recorder with me. I could have used his comments as instructional material on the art of the suck-up.

This gave me an idea. *Why not pretend to quit smoking?*

I now support the most severe restrictions on cigarettes. I roundly condemn Joe Camel. I sold my Philip Morris stock (thank God before the price went down).

In doing this, I have made a lot of new friends, some of

whom have become clients. Yes, they are guardians of moral purity. Yes, they are *boring and predictable*. Yes, they believe me.

You see, people are pouring their legitimate anger at the system into what is at worst a dirty habit. They are feeding their puritanical urges. (H. L. Mencken beautifully defined Puritanism as "the feeling that somewhere, somehow, someone is enjoying himself.")

I say: Divert their attention! If they worry about smokers, they won't worry about ineffective people stealing their money by pretending to work.

To become a tobacco company executive, invert the process: Pretend to smoke and become a pro–tobacco rights militant.

These stratagems are intended only as starting points, as germs that ineffectiveness can grow from—*and prosper.* Once you master at least one or two of these, of your own choosing, other wonderfully wasteful tactics will present themselves, sometimes *without your even knowing it.*

CASE STUDY

Ed McMahon

In many ways, it is impossible to think of a better case study for this last habit than Ed McMahon, who is a real hero to me.

Don't laugh. *He is a hero.* And, by the time you're done with this section, he will be to you, too. Quite simply, he combines most of these final principles for perfecting ineffectiveness.

He has used heavy drinking to advance his career. True, he has not gone through any twelve-step programs, but why bother? He already lives in a city with a warm climate. His work is so undemanding that he can probably do it with a hangover—or even drunk. Who would know the difference? *Why would they care?*

He has used pitiful behavior to further his career, too. Anyone who watched the last few years of *"The Tonight Show,"* under Carson's reign, saw McMahon take some pretty tough swipes from time to time.

On one show, for example, Carson solicited questions from the audience. One spectator allegedly asked (the questions were read by Carson, so who knows where they really came from), "What would happen if you and Ed McMahon were on an airplane that was crashing and there was only one parachute?"

Carson replied, "Your next Publishers Clearinghouse Sweepstakes entry form would come to you from hell."

McMahon *laughed* at this.

Toward the end, it got so bad that when Dana Carvey spoofed Carson on *Saturday Night Live*, he used a *stereo speaker* for the part of Ed McMahon. This speaker barked out metallic laughlike sounds.

As far as I know, McMahon has not used either mistakes or anti–tobacco fervor to advance his career. But why should he?

McMahon is rich. He does work that he has done for so long that he can do it in his sleep, and probably does. He had a nasty divorce, if you believe the supermarket tabloids (which are good sources of information—and even better workplaces—for the ineffective), but he probably has his pick of Southern California beach babes.

And he doesn't even have to be nasty.
He's my hero.

You are now ready to face career hell anew. Armed with this precious knowledge, you will be able to fail upward with amazing confidence. Knock 'em dead! (Or at least pretend to.)

APPENDIX A:
The Seven Habits of Highly Ineffective People Problem and Excuse Guide

The following is a list of ten common problems that confront ineffective people on a daily basis. Each problem is followed by three plausible or at least possible excuses, all of which, in the true spirit of ineffectiveness, deflect attention from the true source of the trouble—*you*.

Together, they amply illustrate and supplement the ineffective habits I have previously outlined.

WARNING: This is *not* a substitute for reading the book. If you are truly ineffective, you certainly want to avoid all work, even the work of reading this slim volume. Nonetheless, you *must* read it. Sorry.

Problem: A bill hasn't been paid in a timely manner.
Excuses:
1. There have been some "changes" in the accounting department.
2. The new computer system has some "glitches."
3. Your assistant mislaid the invoice.

*Problem: Some important market research has not been completed/
has not been written up.*
Excuses:
1. Some "troubling" questions have arisen about the person/
company that did the research. Until you can be assured
about the accuracy of the work, you will not circulate the
material. You are only trying to protect the company and/or
the person who's trying to get you to do your job.
2. You're still waiting for further material/a rival's work/a new
computer.
3. Didn't your assistant already turn in the work?

*Problem: A contract agreed upon weeks or months ago has not been
completed.*
Excuses:
1. There have been some "changes" in the contracts
department.
2. The new computer system tracking deals has some
"glitches."
3. Your assistant misplaced the contract request. There have
been some problems lately, but you've spoken to him/her.

Problem: Your evaluation of _____, *who reports to you, is weeks/
months/years late.*
Excuses:
1. There have been some "problems" lately, and you may
need to revise/rewrite the generally positive, in fact, almost
glowing, appraisal you had completed.
2. The "problems" are so bad that they raise "murky legal
issues" that you may have to approach the company's legal
counsel about, once you've gotten to the bottom of it.
3. Your assistant apparently misplaced the form. How much
more of this can you take?

Problem: Your boss is bothering you to schedule a brainstorming session, which you have delayed in the hopes it will go away. You're not good at brainstorming sessions.

Excuses:

1. Due to recent "changes," you're not sure who to invite. You were just about to ask your boss/_____ for advice.

2. There have been some "glitches" in arranging for a conference room/outside site. All will soon be resolved.

3. Didn't your assistant already forward the suggested invitation list? You'll get to the bottom of this immediately.

Problem: An address list for a very important direct mail promotion is seriously late.

Excuses:

1. There have been some "changes" in the promotions department, but _____ in promotion assures you that they will have it to you soon.

2. There are some "glitches" in the new data base program.

3. Didn't your assistant forward the list already? You're shocked—*shocked*—to hear that the list is late. Round up the usual suspects.

Problem: An important letter has not been received.

Excuses:

1. The U.S. Post Office is unbelievably bad. They should make some "changes."

2. You mailed the letter weeks ago. (Then produce a spurious carbon copy to back up this claim.) Perhaps someone should look into the procedures in the mail room. This isn't the only problem of late. (This is an especially good excuse due to the falsely low opinion most people hold of mail rooms.)

3. You thought your assistant mailed it already. You're getting angry, but you'll remain calm. *This is getting serious.*

Problem: An important report is weeks/months/years late.
Excuses:
1. There have been some "changes," and you are rewriting the report even as we speak.
2. Some "murky" legal issues have arisen.
3. Your assistant still has not properly assembled and prepared the report. You've just about had it.

Problem: A product launch has been delayed due to a late market research report.
Excuses:
1. Due to "changes," you're not sure who to send it to. What do you think? (Thereby putting the responsibility elsewhere.)
2. There have been some "glitches" in putting the final version together. You're *still* waiting for _____'s input.
3. You finally had to fire your assistant. The temp was supposed to take care of this. Now you're going to have to complain to the agency.

Problem: An evaluation of a new site is seriously late.
Excuses:
1. There have been some "changes" in the engineering/design/finance/_____ department(s).
2. Some "serious concerns," potentially raising public relations issues, have come up. The company's real estate broker is really falling down on the job.
3. Didn't the new temp already forward the report? The company really should get a new temp agency. Meanwhile, you're obviously going to have to fire the one you've got.

APPENDIX B:
A Typical Ineffective Day

A.M.

7:00 Alarm goes off.

7:01 Hit snooze button.

7:11 Alarm goes off again.

7:12 Turn alarm off.

8:30 Office opens for business.

8:35 Roll out of bed.

8:37 Take pain reliever.

8:39 Turn on *Today* show.

8:40 Fantasize about Katie Couric, Bryant Gumbel, or even Willard Scott. (Suit yourself.)

8:45 Program VCR to record "Talk Soup."

8:46 Boil water for instant coffee.

8:49 Drink coffee and eat stale chocolate donut.

8:50 Begin shower.

9:00 Get dressed.

9:10 Leave for work.

9:13 Return home to make sure you locked door.

9:55 Dream up story about bad traffic/ mass transit delay. (*Note:* You might call

in a different ex-
cuse, such as a
breakfast meeting,
neighborhood dis-
pute, doctor's
appointment, or the
like, a little after
9:00 A.M., when the
caffeine and sugar
have begun to
work.)

10:03 Walk confidently
into work.

10:07 Shut office door.

10:09 Catnap.

10:24 Check voice mail.

11:00 Deal with any mes-
sage(s) requiring
immediate atten-
tion. Discard other
messages.

11:25 Start thinking se-
riously about lunch.

11:36 Begin project—any
project.

11:58 Stop work and be-
gin preparing for
lunch.

P.M.

12:00 Go to lunch. *Enjoy
it.*

2:00 Go shopping.

2:45 Return to office.

2:55 Grill assistant about
day's work.

3:05 Place personal
phone call. (See
Habit 2 for making
personal calls look
official.)

3:20 Check voice mail.

3:45 Answer any urgent
messages. Discard
others.

4:00 Place another per-
sonal phone call.
Really make it count.

4:15 Resume work.

4:25 Take well-deserved
break.

4:35 Start thinking about
leaving.

4:50 Leave early due to
_____.

5:50 Call assistant and
grill him/her again.
Really get into it.

6:00 Send out for dinner.

6:10 Watch Video tape of
"Talk Soap."

7:10 Plot sabotage of col-
      leagues.
8:00 Hit bars or indulge
      in another vice.
11:00 Don't quit indulging
      yet. *The night is still
      young.*
12:30 Act dignified when
      booted out of bar.
1:00 Catch end of Conan
      O'Brien's show.

      Dream about
      achieving his level
      of ineffectiveness.
1:30 Check station guide
      for adult movies on
      cable.
1:45 Fall asleep on
      couch.
3:45 Take off clothes and
      go to bed.

Note: This is a *particularly* ineffective day. Not all days can be this useless and fun-filled, but, *by keeping this ideally ineffective day in mind*, you will always have a goal to aspire down to.

ABOUT THE AUTHOR

HERMAN MINOR IV is founder and president of Minor Associates, his consulting and billing firm based in our nation's capital. Like his ancestors, he graduated from a major, prestigious university through a remarkable series of clerical errors, which he engineered in his voluminous spare time. In his varied career, Minor has worked in a remarkably large number of jobs in a short period of time, usually escaping before it was too late. In the past ten years, his firm has provided advice to a number of companies, most of which remain in business in spite of their sorry performances. More important, their overpaid senior managements have held on to their ineffective niches. In every case, they have viewed Minor's advice as instrumental, and they have paid through the nose for it. Minor lives with his ineffective wife and children in Washington, D.C., a city he says is "after his own heart."

To produce this work, Minor has employed the services of an editor at a major New York publishing house as a ghost writer.

THE DRIVE FOR INEFFECTIVENESS GOES ON!

My hopes and aspirations for all ineffective people, Americans and foreigners, are boundless. I am also greedy. I am planning a series of books on ineffectiveness. Topics to be covered will include ineffective career development, ineffective government service, ineffective entrepreneurship, ineffective exercise and Zen and ineffectiveness. If you have any ineffective ideas (please be specific), please send them to:

Boxholder
P.O. Box 020367
Brooklyn, NY 11201

If you include your name, address, and (if applicable) pseudonym, you will be credited in some form.

INDEX